T0207562

Global Dreams of
Poetry Forever

Global Dreams of Poetry Forever

GENE B. PACIFICO

Rev. date: 03/12/2019

To order additional copies of this book, contact:
Xlibris
1-888-795-4274
www.Xlibris.com
Orders@Xlibris.com
793794

CONTENTS

In loving memory of my mother Dolores June Pacifico

Family, and many friends

TREASURES IN THE DEEPEST OF THE SEA

By Eugene B. Pacifico

When we meet each other
Giving a chance to one another
One love begun.
Having fun at the beach of joy.
Take a walk together
In all types of weather.
Where we'll find our treasures
In the deepest phantoms of the sea

THOSE SPECIAL WORDS

By Eugene B. Pacifico

A picture is worth A thousand words. So I heard.
But such pretty words
In all the world.
Is a Special I love you
From Mom and Dad.

OUT TO SEE

By Eugene B. Pacifico

The days of tomorrow.
When they come to an end.
I suppose that you bring
forward. Warm words to
pretend.
I sit by the pond
With my line out to see.
She caught a big rainbow trout.
That what a friend brings to me.

DREAM OF TOMORROW

By Eugene B. Pacifico

I laid down to rest
under the covers to sleep.
To dream of tomorrow.
Unsullied to dream.
I dreamed of an angel
that coyly spoke to me
Who told me tomorrow?
I will rest with Thee

A KING THAT WAS ABLE

By Eugene B. Pacifico

To live for a day.
In the life of a King.
Would bring quite joy and
astonishing well being
But wouldn't it be better
To bring to the table.
All that was meant
for As you are able.

BE A CHAMP

By Eugene B. Pacifico

Take a chance
To be a champ
The choir will sing along
Be a friend
Forgive again
For Peace is always welcome in the end

SUNNY DAY'S

By Eugene B.Pacifico

The skys so blue
Not a cloud of
gray Today is special
In so many way's
You told me you love me
I told you the same
In this moment of each sunny day.

GODS SPECIAL LOVE

By Eugene B. Pacifico

In the mystic midnight blooms The
cosmic stars of the universe
Shining on and on throught the planets
Why not say hello to all those who rest in their souls
The people of earth need to know
What brings us life is the sparkle of the stars
And brings us upward and onward
On our way to the heavens
Where our lifes continue to exist
In the end of nowhere where
In infinity life is aglow
With God's Special Love

FEELINGS

By Eugene B. Pacifico

Inside looking out
I stand before you
With words I cannot say
What I am feeling is
Life cast in the shadows
Locked in foggy mist of the day
As time locked in a casement on stage
I wonder what brought upon you
The rage you will today
I hope that it rains long again
To unlock the fire of your words
And please the god of Fire within
That you touch the warmth of the sun
To feel the breath of cool mist from the sea
Let it touch your heart
And smile again
Yes I know its only a matter of time

DREAMS THAT NEVER FADE AWAY

Eugene B. Pacifco

Once upon a time in nowhere land
There was this little chance
To make it big in life
But I never frayed and dismissed
This obligation swiftly went astray
But I have a bigger chance for even more
On each and everyday
To play the game in life
Like no other guy could even dream
You see there are a billion of stars in the sky
And each one belongs to us
All you have to do is trust yourself
And one will be on the way

DAYS TRUE BLUE

By Eugene B. Pacifico

The days of today are blue
But in a good ways that are new
Sometimes I wonder how could
All of todays people have good news
Could it be because we are all true blue
We will never tell a lie
That would get us all in trouble
If we never blew a day off
As sometime we do
That would mean to everone
Each day we knew
Would be a good as new
Of we True blue people
Carved by our lives so blue
The Wonderful World so
Beautiful as we ever new

Everyday we make each day
A day in the experience we all know
To be just like the won we do
Would we ever know?

ENGULFED IN MY HEART FOREVER

By Eugene B. Pacifico

A soft peddle of a rose
A small tiny emblem of remembrance
The summer, fall, winter, spring
Could dance in the wind
Or lay on a pond, river, lake,
Or drift with the breeze
Under your nose to say hello
This will make you sparkle and smile?
But a wonderful experience
To touch the beauty and Feel
the depth or wonder Where
the seeds of life began
To find a wonderful dance in the heart
Of you in the deepness
To re-enter our lives Emerald forest searching
For a moment where love encumbers
The dance of your lovely rose pedal
Engulfed in my heart for
A soft peddle of a rose
A small tiny emblem of remembrance

YOU AS A CHILD

By Eugene B. Pacifico

The tweak of the night light
Twinkling on the flick of
Jack on a candle stick
Wittingly should a voice be heard?
Announcing the presense on the past
I carnival, a fair, a circus clown
A cannon blast with the sound That
resonances with the laughter With
the bliss of a triumphant voice
Which seethes through on the pure white shore
Of crystals of clandestine sand on
Disneyland's Snow Whites beach
Which invites the silence to allow
What a wonderful life it is to have
The marionette of joy to see
The visions as to have smiled with
You as a child

WHAT A SONG IS SUNG

By Eugene B. Pacifico

I believe you will hear
A thousand times in the sea mist
That the world will rejoice
When we cajole on the sea roof
Intrigue where one miss
As we tide on warm waters
To idle under the Midnight moon
You are dancing with the
King of your heart

The Joke that Spoke Enjoyed Me

By Eugene B. Pacifico

The solitude of time
Confines me in rhymes
Non one anywhere can find me
An explicit joke
One that has just spoke
Entwine with antiques
To evoke me
I have no spell
Going to stay out of hell
May the Holy Ghost find me
Then I will say
Going to find a way
The joke that spoke enjoyed me

COSMOS OF ETERNITY

By Eugene B. Pacifco

Someday it seems
All the trees are green
Solitude of the sun warms me
Although their my sometimes be rain
Your love will always endure me
When you say hello
I mean to show
All there is in life bestows
With the drowning of my soul
Come walk with my heart
Touch the sun and the moon
Will announce it spirts
In its part of the will as we burst
into the cosmos of eternity

YOUR OPEN DOOR OF LOVE

By Eugene B. Pacifico

When you open the door
Say no more
The hallow of your spirits
Come join me
As once before
Not only by the shore
Your song of love sang mystically
Cool whispering breeze
Once again through magical trees
On this day never to part
And wait her patiently
Until I find your door of love
Opened eternally

BECAUSE OF YOU

By Eugene B. Pacifico

Because of you
The Road again
So Bold and tempest rule
I make a gesture
To ride and capture
The road ahead
Is paved with gold

SOLUTUDE AND GRACE

By Eugene B. Pacifico

Since the beginning of time
I waste no time
The strike of the blade
Has saved me
In the nick of time
My words all rhyme
And solitude and grace
has found me

THE MORNING SUN

By Eugene B. Pacifico

The morning sun
Fills the sky with dreams
And sources to displace
The gray and rainy days in life
But one day I will always remember
That is the sight of the flight
That shook up the night
And turned on the moonlight
Under the stars to more of
The tomorrow sunlights.

PONY'S ROAD TO FOREVER

By Eugene B. Pacifico

The clock strike twelve
And the mouse lost its tail
The moon shining everywhere after
Twas the night of the red barn owl
Prowled of the ground
And the pony's trolleyed
On the road to forever

A WALK IN THE PARK IN MY BABY'S ARMS

By Eugent B. Pacifico

Got up this morning
Shaved washed my face and hands
In the sink don't you think?
That the soap was a link
To the slipery and shining
Soapy suds filled with love
Turning my nightmares to end
And merrily dance with the
Glow of the suns feelings
To lick up my thoughts
As clean as a cat
And pure in my heart
as a walk in the park
In my baby's arms.

YESTERDAY'S DREAMS

By Eugene B. Pacifco

Take a chance
Make a glance
In the mirror
Of eternal love
Maybe you'll find
A doorway to your dreams
And softly
You will remember me

STARS OF AMERICA

By Eugnene B. Pacifico

In the misty moonlight
Away in the depths of the sea
There is a ghost ship sailing
Wandering through history
Remembering all the wars
The battle of the seas
Sometimes I sit and wonder
Did the Stars of America
Come that way we see

MUSIC OF SYMMETRIC TRILOGY

In this spectacular World of art
I got a shot at show business
The choir echoed with
The words of love
And no more tears have brought life
Through the years
And my triumphant audience
As the show moves on
The crowds awaits me
Bring open the curtains
The show is on
The music is as sure
As the angels more far
Singing encompassing all hearts
In our symmetric trilogy

THERE WAS A CANNON BLASTING

By Eugene B. Pacifico

Away in the far
The gods Zeus and Thor contemplate
The destruction we saw
We see the tragic devasty
The silence of the storm
The mighty river floodiing
All those who do us harm
But who they are the evildoers
Who wreak haven to us all
Will always be remembered
By our blasting cannons
Thunder and Roar.

WALKING TO
TOMORROW'S WILL

By Eugene B. Pacifico

The beauty of the day
Is watching from a satellite
The TV news
Where everyone knows
And everythings goes
Into a prism of eternal light
To see or remember someone
Always walking on the bridges will
Of memories of the tomorrows

LOVE AS THE ROSES

By Eugene B. Pacifico

It's cloudy and grey today
All the the sunshine has gone away
It probably will rain
To ease the pain
And open a window
To view the world in hope
If the ocean of the worlds solitude
Will humanly seek
To light a candle
That the sun will take
To spread the warmth
That the Roses will breath
And the people will love
As God above.

PEACE

By Eugene B. Pacifico

A moment of inspiration
That all our renown nation
Can feel the sounds
Of missiles infernal
Firing from the ground
With The words of War
That is will exist no more
And Peace will
Conquer the land
Throughout all Nations.

SWORD OF MY SANCTURARY

By Eugene B. Pacifco

I haven't to think
That my mind is on the blink
Theres no one nowhere to guide me
I look to the stars
And rage my sword
To thank the Lord
Who has saved me?
Of you in the
Sancturary of my heart forever

A GIFT

By Eugene B. Pacifico

A wonderful gift
Is waiting for us
Under the wings of a Saint
An angel with a halo
And wings that soar
Are waiting at heaven's door
Eternal love granted

PRECIOUS WORDS

By Eugene B. Pacifico

A picture is worth a thousand words
So I heard
But such pretty words
In all the world
Is a Special I love you
From Mom and Dad

LOVE AS DEEP AS THE SEAS

By Eugene B. Pacifico

When we meet each other
Giving the chance of another
One lfe to share
One love begun
Having fun
At the beach of joy
Take a walk together
In all types of weather
Where we'll find
Our arts and treasure
In our hearts
Under the depths
Of the phantoms of the seas

WHAT A FRIEND BRINGS TO ME

By Eugene B. Pacifico

The days of tomorrow
When they come to an end
I suppose that you'll bring forward
Words never to pretend
I sit by the pond
With my line out to see
She caught a big rainbow trout
That's what a friend brings to me

Gift's of Tomorrow's

By Eugene B. Pacifico

In a day of solitude to remember
All the sweet times in life
To ask for the giving
And say its nice to be filled with life
A day to repose
And don't you suppose
The gifts of all the tomorrows will dwell

MARRIED TO THE GODS

By Eugene B. Pacifico

Please let me be the honor
To bring the earths vine of wine and roses
To bestow to you here
As the rarest of all angles charismatically sing
A song of love and cheer
That this is the moment
So desirably calculated and near
Our will bring us closer
To the gold, diamond and emearld Chalice of the gods
Both Zeus and Thor will cheer
The thunder and clamor of volcanoes
And the earth Quakes
The moment we we wed is here
Our hearts are one with the universe my dear.

THE COSMIC SUN

By Eugene B. Pacifico

This is a thought of a memory of fading glory
You stood and glared with eyes of fiery glaze
Who's tool the sword which pirerced the heart
Of solitude and dispair
To bring a compromise to the thoughts of present
Where those who perished
Will become one with our universe
To feel the tone of your sword
That evildoers will reign no more
And those memories will
become loved by everyone
In the blessed times of repose
For those who died will live
And no one will perish no more
In the New World in the warmth of the Cosmic Sun

My 56ᵀᴴ Birthday Phenomenal Panegyric

By Eugene B. Pacifico

Love is good and love is real
Was I to kiss your lips like it was
Our very first time
Sunshine all day from the morning birth
Illusions of dancing swallowing sandpipers
Endless flight in the Moonlight mirror aglow
Mirth amused by the virtuoso on the sea in the evening
Our love is circling the earth
In a human vessel of flesh and blood
As ole glory waves in the breeze
It's my 56th silver mountain heavenly Birthday
As old as the oaks feel high
Or like a cloud in the dark midnight mist
Searching for the love of enchanted hallows
Where there is no end to our vessels of
Words of rhyme sycnchronized in our time
On this supernatural moments
In history with our hearts rhythm we see
The majestical magic trip on the crimson ship
Accross our minds starlite
Your eyes deep in magical prismatic color

Psychedelic Rainbows rays rhyme
With cosmic showers of our love
Like the scintillating sun beems rays of light
On the sea crest of waves tides of energy
Where in the snowy oceans sands of depth
Our hypnotic eyes will always meet
As for when our hearts touched
Blessed and distilled once in a
lifetime Now life moves on
And love begins again
That cannot be changed
Forever enchanted by the galloping winds
In our history on time
These words we left behind
I never will let you down And mess you around
Our minds are images that mirrors visages of God
Reflecting our deep visual images on our souls
Our love is delved in our enchanting minds
Where our cotton seeds fly
Over the double rainbows
To spawn a child to birth
In the hearts of the universe
Who live in God's love
Of our spirtual spiraling welcome forever
In the world of the Magical Majestic wonders
who Forever loves our Promise Land
So please take me on a magic ride
Accross the universe
I want to have this birthday wish

From my heart whispered by
The touch of the arch of sun
Welcomed aglow with the intense
Wishes and dreams who always come true
Every time I think of you
My phenominal panegyrice birthday lover

SOMEONE WHISPERING IN THE WIND

By Eugene B. Pacifico

The glow of the sunlight is everywhere
Where did the doom and gloom appear
To someone so very dear
Look away in the night somewhere
In the heart the glare of darkness has struck
Someone who wasn't meant to beware
Of the miser who laughter insanely screaming
The end of a night of honor is bestowed
In the wisdom of the cilvilization he lived in
So the sunlight lit of the hearts and minds
Surrounded by prismatic rainbows who sang
By Nightingales whispering in the wind
Aglow the time is not near but far away
We will ever see a song in the wind
Capturing the hearts and lives of everyone
Dancing like a whispering willow tree
In the enchanted forest where
The night of honor life long songs sung
Where did the gloom and doom go
Blessed by the words of all religions
Where in the end and his new life ghostly abridges

The nightengales of past and in present into our reality
Glow spiral rays of the sun is sung again
In the hearts of the voices of civilizations
Where the spiritual seed of his life returns
To give birth to someone whispering in the wind
Words of the nightengales impetuous beauty, "The sun"

OLD BUT SEE SOMEONE

By Eugene B. Pacifico

So you think you had just all you can take.
\It seems like each day you're second rate.
\The skies turn gray and prismatic sun
\bursts through the galaxies one by one.
\Guiding you home to new life begun
\and you are the superhero to a new day's dawn.
\You discover you are really someone.

WINTER FADES TO SURRENDER TO THE SUN

By Eugene B. Pacifico

Winter frost enters the twilight midnight stars
Swirling snow in storms of gallant heroic force
Dancing like a flamingo flying home to its breed
To there-hence brings the revolving sun
Amongst the stars to embrace the springs spirit
Who's presence brings the warmth of the summer's heat
To enhance the lovers hearts and sing
It's rainbow colors of prismatic beauty
who's kisses
Bring the changes of time where forth the bells
Of Notra Dame dwell in the trade-winds of
Civilization's.

FIRST WINTER LOVE

By Eugene B. Pacifico

She told your a hero
Her knight in shining armor
Midnight showers of shooting
Stars across the universe
Endless winter stormy night
Lovingly each touch prismatic
Words of breath, snow, and slush
Dancing unforgiven with the moon
She is now one with the sun
And her stance
Is like the
Swirling cosmic
Of rainbow's toung
Dreaming beneath you in awe

HAPPY BIRTHDAY CARA

By Eugene B. Pacifico

Cotton valley's and blue bells
Dancing in the moonlight
Enchanting choirs of angels sing
Amongst the sea's shore cocker shells
The misty morning of seagulls
Almost touch the sun
The song has been so gratefully sung
The dawn of day that she brings
Engulfed by the seducing twilight stars
Bursting to light and guiding home
Where the angels bring
In each time begun
Where has the thought
Of newborn life beg
It's time again for Cara's
Bright and marvelous Birthday.

IN SLUMBER BETWEEN THE SHEETS

By Eugene B. Pacifico

Twos the flight of the prancing
\midnight owl
\Unto the unfortunate but
\permissively luscious
\Is this of when the rainbow of still
\yet the glamorous colors dancing in
\the sunshine
\Of the moonlight between the
\twilight and the dawn
\To the flamingo's Walt's with time
\and the distance to give
\The owls prancing flight between the
\starlight and the twilight
\Invincibly and invisible to her to
\be unknown
\The owls consummately conspicuous
\but happy glow
\When the dance of the flamingo yet
\still prancing down on her sun

MAGICAL GARDENS

By Eugene B. Pacifco

Cotton bells and chocker shells
\And fields of cotton candy
\I will bring my love to you
\And whisper in your ear
\Candy canes and blissful years
\Of seashells and ocean sea orchids
\Dream of me and I'll be there
\to share my love in your deepest forest
\Carousels and magical spells of sky's of prismatic colors
\My dreams come true and I love you
\Till the end of twilight stars and magical gardens

AWARE OF HER LOVELINESS

By Eugene B. Pacifico

Don't be blamed for you incospicuous lust of her hell
\She was the women who was meant to be
\Cast to the sea in her humble abode
\To seek out the octopuses garden way below
\The depths of her mysterious mind will swallow thee
\For the day has come to discover
\The majestic twilight of the harvest moon
\Dwelling in the souls of all mankind
\To be one with the one in the house of the holy
\Where all her love is prolific and dwell
\And cast away to the Bermuda triangle
\Where the blissfull days of copulation are blinded by the
\Opulent white lights of the gateway to euphoria

BEGINNINGS FROM PAST GHOST OF LOVE

By Eugene B. Pacifico

Once beyond a presipice moon
\The dandelion spoke of her perspective song
\The love she lost has now been reborn
\Rehabed and rejuvenated at last forever at this doorstep
\With millions of stars in the depth of the house of the holy
\To join in the choir with the children of the universe
\To be amongst the twilight spawning a mystical moon
\To dance her song to the choir of the solace sun
\For a new beginning of liveing a song of love has begun.

LOVE

By Eugene B. Pacifco

Sole priortorships amonog the mast
\of masterful ships
\Toward the end of all destines
\We build the future generations.
\You must encompass our conveyance to
\the building
\Who renounce the never-ending
\majestic kingdoms
\Of diamond, gold, silver, and ore
\Built with the toil, an ominous peril
\dwelling
\In the souls of the prestigious
\omnipotent wells.
\To be brought to the children of
\the universe.
\We watch the Creator of existence.
\Who is the world?

Printed in the United States
By Bookmasters